Holy Spirit: The Helper

By Shantae Bolden

Dear Parents,

This book is intended to be a tool to help introduce your child to the Holy Spirit. At the end of the book there are scriptural references for each illustration. Please feel free to use these scriptures as teaching points for your older children. I pray this book is a blessing to you.

Holy Spirit: The Helper

Copyright © 2019 by Shantae Bolden— All Rights Reserved

All rights reserved. No part of this book may be reproduced or transmitted in any form or by any means without written permission from the Author.

ISBN: 978-0-578-45623-2

Printed in USA

Hi! My name is Holy Spirit!

I was sent by God to be a gift for you.

You can take me wherever you go!

My favorite thing to do is to help people!
I want to show you all the ways I can help you.
LET'S GO!

I can help you pray!

Dear God, thank you for loving me.
Thank you for being my friend.
Thank you for making me special.
Thank you for your help.
I love you so much! In Jesus name I pray. Amen!

I can help you make tough choices.

I can help you when you feel sad.

I can help you learn cool things about God!

God makes birds sing.

God makes the flowers grow.

God makes the sun shine. Hello Sun!

I can teach you about my friend Jesus!
Jesus loves you!
Jesus is your friend too!

**Even though you can't see me,
I'm always there living in your heart.**

**Do YOU want me to be your special Helper?
Say this prayer with me:**

Holy Spirit, I want you to help me. I want you to live inside my heart. Thank you for being my friend. I love you Holy Spirit! In Jesus name I pray. Amen!

The End

For Parents:

Scriptural References

- "Tough choices"- Ephesians 1:17
- "When you feel afraid"- II Timothy 2:17
- "Cool things about God" - John 14:26
- "My friend Jesus" - John 14:26
- "Living in your heart" - I Corinthians 6:19

Made in the USA
Monee, IL
12 January 2020